To

From

Date

THE *Cross*

INSPIRATION FOR EVERYDAY LIFE

MAX LUCADO

THOMAS NELSON
Since 1798

Published in Nashville, Tennessee, by Thomas Nelson. Thomas Nelson is a registered trademark of HarperCollins Christian Publishing, Inc.

Thomas Nelson titles may be purchased in bulk for educational, business, fund-raising, or sales promotional use. For information, please e-mail SpecialMarkets@ThomasNelson.com.

Library of Congress Cataloging-in-Publication Data

ISBN 978-0-7180-9136-1

Printed in China

17 18 19 20 21 RRD 10 9 8 7 6 5 4 3 2 1

And being found in

appearance as a man,

he *humbled* himself by

becoming *obedient*

to death— even death

on a *cross!*

—Philippians 2:8 (NIV)

The cross.

It rests on the time line of history like a compelling diamond. Its tragedy summons all sufferers. Its absurdity attracts all cynics. Its hope lures all searchers.

And according to Paul, the cross is what counts.

My, what a piece of wood! History has idolized it and despised it, gold-plated it and burned it, worn and trashed it. History has done everything to it but ignore it.

That's the one option that the cross does not offer.

No one can ignore it! You can't ignore a piece of lumber that suspends the greatest claim in history. A crucified carpenter claiming that he is God on earth? Divine? Eternal? The death slayer?

No wonder Paul called it "the core of the gospel." Its bottom line is sobering: if the account is true, it is history's hinge. Period. If not, it is history's hoax.

That's why the cross is what matters.

—NO WONDER THEY CALL HIM THE SAVIOR

The diadem of pain,
which sliced your gentle face,
three spikes piercing flesh and wood
to hold you in your place.
The need for blood I understand.
Your sacrifice I embrace.
But the bitter sponge, the cutting spear,
the spit upon your face?

Did it have to be a cross?
Did not a kinder death exist
than six hours hanging between life and death,
all spurred by a betrayer's kiss?
"Oh, Father," you pose,
heart-stilled at what could be,
"I'm sorry to ask, but I long to know,
did you do this for me?"

—He Chose the Nails

Like a master painter God reserved his masterpiece until the end. All the earlier acts of love had been leading to this one. The angels hushed and the heavens paused to witness the finale. God unveils the canvas and the ultimate act of creative compassion is revealed.

God on a cross.

The Creator being sacrificed for the creation. God convincing man once and for all that forgiveness still follows failure.

I wonder if, while on the cross, the Creator allowed his thoughts to wander back to the beginning. One wonders if he allowed the myriad of faces and acts to parade in his memory. Did he reminisce about the creation of the sky and sea? Did he relive the conversations with Abraham and Moses? Did he remember the plagues and the promises, the wilderness and the wanderings? We don't know.

We do know, however, what he said.

"It is finished."

The mission was finished. All that the master painter needed to do was done and was done in splendor. His creation could now come home.

"It is finished!" he cried.

And the great Creator went home.

(He's not resting, though. Word has it that his tireless hands are preparing a city so glorious that even the angels get goose bumps upon seeing it. Considering what he has done so far, that is one creation I plan to see.)

—No Wonder They Call Him the Savior

Nails didn't

hold *God*

to a cross.

Love did.

—When God Whispers Your Name

The Anchor Points of the Cross

Six hours, one Friday.

To the casual observer the six hours are mundane. A shepherd with his sheep, a housewife with her thoughts, a doctor with his patients. But to the handful of awestruck witnesses, the most maddening of miracles is occurring.

God is on a cross. The creator of the universe is being executed.

Spit and blood are caked to his cheeks, and his lips are cracked and swollen. Thorns rip his scalp. His lungs scream with pain. His legs knot with cramps. Taut nerves threaten to snap as pain twangs her morbid melody. Yet, death is not ready. And there is no one to save him, for he is sacrificing himself.

It is no normal six hours. . . . it is no normal Friday.

Far worse than the breaking of his body is the shredding of his heart.

His own countrymen clamored for his death.

His own disciple planted the kiss of betrayal.

His own friends ran for cover.

And now his own father is beginning to turn his back on him, leaving him alone.

A witness could not help but ask: Jesus, do you give no thought to saving yourself? What keeps you there? What holds you to the cross? Nails don't hold gods to trees. What makes you stay?

Six hours. One Friday.

Let me ask you a question: What do you do with that day in history? What do you do with its claims?

If it really happened . . . if God did commandeer his own crucifixion . . . if he did turn his back on his own son . . . if he did storm Satan's gate, then those six hours that Friday were packed

with tragic triumph. If that was God on that cross, then the hill called Skull is granite studded with stakes to which you can anchor.

Those six hours were no normal six hours. They were the most critical hours in history. For during those six hours on that Friday, God embedded in the earth three anchor points sturdy enough to withstand any hurricane.

Anchor point #1—*My life is not futile.* This rock secures the hull of your heart. Its sole function is to give you something that you can grip when facing the surging tides of futility and relativism. It's a firm grasp on the conviction that there is truth.

Someone is in control and you have a purpose.

Anchor point #2—*My failures are not fatal.* It's not that he loves what you did, but he loves who you are. You are his. The One who has the right to condemn you provided the way to acquit you. You make mistakes. God doesn't. And he made you.

Anchor point #3—*My death is not final.* There is one more stone to which you should tie. It's large. It's round. And it's heavy. It blocked the door of a grave. It wasn't big enough, though. The tomb that it sealed was the tomb of a transient. He only went in to prove he could come out. And on the way out he took the stone with him and turned it into an anchor point. He dropped it deep into the uncharted waters of death. Tie to his rock and the typhoon of the tomb becomes a spring breeze on Easter Sunday.

There they are. Three anchor points. The anchor points of the cross.

—Six Hours One Friday

My life is not *futile.*

My failures are not *fatal.*

My death is not *final.*

The One who has the right to condemn you provided the way to acquit you. You make mistakes. God doesn't. And he made you.

There was something about the crucifixion that made every witness either step toward it or away from it. It simultaneously compelled and repelled.

And today, two thousand years later, the same is true. It's the watershed. It's the Continental Divide. It's Normandy. And you are either on one side or the other. A choice is demanded. We can do what we want with the cross. We can examine its history. We can study its theology. We can reflect upon its prophecies. Yet the one thing we can't do is walk away in neutral. No fence sitting is permitted. The cross, in its absurd splendor, doesn't allow that. That is one luxury that God, in his awful mercy, doesn't permit.

On which side are you?

—No Wonder They Call Him the Savior

The *sinless* One took on the face of a sinner so that we sinners could take on the face of a *saint.*

—He Chose the Nails

Our Master lived a three-dimensional life. He had as clear a view of the future as he did of the present and the past.

This is why the ropes used to tie his hands and the soldiers used to lead him to the cross were unnecessary. They were incidental. Had they not been there, had there been no trial, no Pilate and no crowd, the very same crucifixion would have occurred. Had Jesus been forced to nail himself to the cross, he would have done it. For it was not the soldiers who killed him, nor the screams of the mob. It was his devotion to us.

So call it what you wish: An act of grace. A plan of redemption. A martyr's sacrifice. But whatever you call it, don't call it an accident. It was anything but that.

—God Came Near

The Hands of Jesus

Oh, the hands of Jesus. Hands of incarnation at his birth. Hands of liberation as he healed. Hands of inspiration as he taught. Hands of dedication as he served. And hands of salvation as he died.

The crowd at the cross concluded that the purpose of the pounding was to skewer the hands of Christ to a beam. But they were only half-right. We can't fault them for missing the other half. They couldn't see it. But Jesus could. And heaven could. And we can.

Through the eyes of Scripture we see what others missed but what Jesus saw. "He canceled the record that contained the charges against us. He took it and destroyed it by nailing it to Christ's cross" (Col. 2:14 NLT).

Between his hand and the wood there was a list. A long list. A list of our mistakes: our lusts and lies and greedy moments and prodigal years. A list of our sins.

Dangling from the cross is an itemized catalog of your sins. The bad decisions from last year. The bad attitudes from last week. There, in broad daylight for all of heaven to see, is a list of your mistakes.

God has done with us what I am doing with our house. He has penned a list of our faults. The list God has made, however, cannot be

read. The words can't be deciphered. The mistakes are covered. The sins are hidden. Those at the top are hidden by his hand; those down the list are covered by his blood. Your sins are "blotted out" by Jesus (see KJV). "He has forgiven you all your sins: Christ has utterly wiped out the damning evidence of broken laws and commandments which always hung over our heads, and has completely annulled it by nailing it over his own head on the cross" (Col. 2:14 PHILLIPS).

This is why he refused to close his fist. He saw the list! What kept him from resisting? This warrant, this tabulation of your failures. He knew the price of those sins was death. He knew the source of those

sins was you, and since he couldn't bear the thought of eternity without you, he chose the nails.

The hand squeezing the handle was not a Roman infantryman.

The force behind the hammer was not an angry mob.

The verdict behind the death was not decided by jealous Jews.

Jesus himself chose the nails.

So the hands of Jesus opened up. Had the soldier hesitated, Jesus himself would have swung the mallet. He knew how; he was no stranger to the driving of nails. As a carpenter he knew what it took. And as a Savior he knew what it meant. He knew that the purpose of the nail

was to place your sins where they could be hidden by his sacrifice and covered by his blood.

So Jesus himself swung the hammer.

The same hand that stilled the seas stills your guilt.

The same hand that cleansed the Temple cleanses your heart.

The hand is the hand of God.

The nail is the nail of God.

And as the hands of Jesus opened for the nail, the doors of heaven opened for you.

—He Chose the Nails

The same *hand* that
stilled the seas stills your
guilt.

The same hand that
cleansed the Temple
cleanses your *heart.*
And as the hands of
Jesus opened for the nail,
the doors of *heaven*
opened for you.

He knew the price of those sins was death. He knew the source of those sins was you, and since he couldn't bear the thought of eternity without you, he chose the nails.

Paul said, "The cross of our Lord Jesus Christ is my only reason for bragging" (Gal. 6:14 NCV). Do you feel a need for affirmation? Does your self-esteem need attention? You don't need to drop names or show off. You need only pause at the base of the cross and be reminded of this: The maker of the stars would rather die for you than live without you. And that is a fact. So if you need to brag, brag about that.

—Traveling Light

The centurion's convictions began to flow together like rivers. "This was no carpenter," he spoke under his breath. "This was no peasant. This was no normal man."

He stood and looked around at the rocks that had fallen and the sky that had blackened. He turned and stared at the soldiers as they stared at Jesus with frozen faces. He turned and watched as the eyes of Jesus lifted and looked toward home. He listened as the parched lips parted and the swollen tongue spoke for the last time.

"Father, into your hands I commit my spirit." (Luke 23:46 NIV)

Had the centurion not said it, the soldiers would have. Had the centurion not said it, the rocks would have—as would have the angels, the stars, even the demons. But he did say it. It fell to a nameless foreigner to state what they all knew.

"Surely he was the Son of God." (Matthew 27:54 NIV)

Six hours on one Friday. Six hours that jut up on the plain of human history like Mount Everest in a desert. Six hours that have been deciphered, dissected, and debated for two thousand years.

What do these six hours signify? They claim to be the door in time through which eternity entered man's darkest caverns. They mark the moments that the Navigator descended into the deepest waters to leave anchor points for his followers.

What does that Friday mean?

For the life blackened with failure, that Friday means forgiveness.

For the heart scarred with futility, that Friday means purpose.

And for the soul looking into this side of the tunnel of death, that Friday means deliverance.

Six hours. One Friday.

What do *you* do with those six hours on that Friday?

—Six Hours One Friday

Jesus once and for all displayed his *authority* over savagery. Evil may have her moments, but they will be *brief.* Satan unleashed his meanest demons on God's Son. He tortured every nerve ending and inflicted every misery. Yet the master of death could not *destroy* the Lord of life. Heaven's best took hell's worst and turned it into *hope.*

—Fearless

Could it be that the two *crosses* on the hill symbolize one of God's greatest gifts? The gift of *choice.*

—He Chose the Nails

The cross will not lose its *power.* The blood of Christ will not *fade* in *strength.* Heaven will never announce the collapse of the bridge. God will never return to the drawing board.

—It's Not About Me

I'm thinking that we aren't so unlike those soldiers at the cross. (I'm sorry to say.)

We, too, play games at the foot of the cross. We compete for members. We scramble for status. We deal out judgments and condemnations. Competition. Selfishness. Personal gain. It's all there. We don't like what the other did so we take the sandal we won and walk away in a huff.

So close to the timber yet so far from the blood.

We are so close to the world's most uncommon event, but we act like common crapshooters huddled in bickering groups and fighting over silly opinions.

How many pulpit hours have been wasted on preaching the trivial? How many churches have tumbled at the throes of miniscuity? How many leaders have saddled their pet peeves, drawn their swords of bitterness and launched into battle against brethren over issues that are not worth discussing?

So close to the cross but so far from the Christ.

We specialize in "I am right" rallies. We write books about what the other does wrong. We major in finding gossip and become experts in unveiling weaknesses. We split into little huddles and then, God forbid, we split again.

Another name. Another doctrine. Another "error." Another denomination. Another poker game. Our Lord must be amazed.

"Those selfish soldiers," we smirk with our thumbs in lapels. "They were so close to the cross and yet so far from the Christ." And yet, are we so different? Our divisions are so numerous that we can't be

cataloged. There are so many offshoots that even the offshoots have shoots!

Now . . . really.

Are our differences that divisive? Are our opinions that obtrusive? Are our walls that wide? Is it *that* impossible to find a common cause?

"May they all be one," Jesus prayed.

One. Not one in groups of two thousand. But one in One. *One* church. *One* faith. *One* Lord. Not Baptist, not Methodist, not Adventist. Just Christians. No denominations. No hierarchies. No traditions. Just Christ.

Too idealistic? Impossible to achieve? I don't think so. Harder things have been done, you know. For example, once upon a tree, a Creator gave his life for his creation. Maybe all we need are a few hearts that are willing to follow suit.

What about you? Can you build a bridge? Toss a rope? Span a chasm? Pray for oneness? Can you be the soldier who snaps to his senses, jumps to his feet, and reminds the rest of us, "Hey, that's God on that cross!"

—No Wonder They Call Him the Savior

Once upon a
tree, a Creator
gave his *life* for
his creation.

Which is easier for Jesus? To forgive a soul or heal a body? Which caused Jesus less pain—providing a man with health or providing a man with heaven?

To heal the man's body took a simple command; to forgive the man's sins took Jesus' blood. The first was done in the house of friends; the second on a hill with thieves. One took a word; the other took his body. One took a moment; the other took his life.

Which was easier?

So strong was his love for a crew of faith that he went beyond their appeal and went straight to the cross.

Jesus already knows the cost of grace. He already knows the price of forgiveness. But he offers it anyway. Love burst his heart.

By the way, he hasn't changed. What happened then happens today. When we take a step of faith, God sees. The same face that beamed at the paralytic beams at the alcoholic refusing the bottle. The same eyes that danced at the friends dance at the mom and dad who will do whatever it takes to get their child to Jesus. And the same lips that spoke to the man in Capernaum speak to the man in Detroit, to the

woman in Belfast, to the child in Moscow . . . to any person anywhere who dares to come into the presence of God and ask for help.

And though we can't hear it here, the angels can hear him there. All of heaven must pause as another burst of love declares the only words that really matter: "Your sins are forgiven."

—He Still Moves Stones

Can you imagine your final message to those you love? Your last words with a child or spouse?

What would you say? How would you say it?

Even if you can't answer the first question, you can answer the second. How would you say your final words? Deliberately. Carefully. Wouldn't you go as Monet to a palette—searching for, not just the right color, but the perfect shade, the exact hue? Most of us have only one chance to make our last statement.

That's all Jesus was given. Knowing his last deeds would be forever pondered, don't you think he chose them carefully? Deliberately? Of course he did. There were no accidents that day. Jesus' last moments were not left up to chance. God chose the path; he selected the nails. Our Lord planted the trio of crosses and painted the sign. God was never more sovereign than in the details of the death of his Son. Your Father left this message:

"I did it for you. I did it all for you."

—He Chose the Nails

God was

never more

sovereign

than in the

details of the

death of

his Son.

Don't all of us live with a fear of the unknown? Don't all of us dread the horrible day when the thin curtain that separates us from evil might be pulled back and in we would tumble? Cancer. Murder. Death. How haunting is that gnawing awareness that we are not immune to life's mishaps and perils.

It's this eerie inconsistency that keeps all of us, to one degree or another, living our lives on the edge of our chairs.

Yet, it was in this inconsistency that God had his finest hour. Never did the obscene come so close to the holy as it did on Calvary. Never did the good in the world so intertwine with the bad as it did on the cross. Never did what is right involve itself so intimately with what is wrong, as it did when Jesus was suspended between heaven and earth.

God on a cross. Humanity at its worst. Divinity at its best.

Something is said at the cross about inconsistencies. Something hopeful. Something healing. Simply stated, that which is consistent did battle with that which is inconsistent, and the consistent won.

Something is also said about God himself. God is not stumped by

an evil world. He doesn't gasp in amazement at the depth of our faith or the depth of our failures. We can't surprise God with our cruelties. He knows the condition of the world . . . and loves it just the same. For just when we find a place where God would never be (like on a cross), we look again and there he is, in the flesh.

—No Wonder They Call Him the Savior

Jesus' death was not the result of a panicking, cosmological engineer. The cross wasn't a tragic surprise. Calvary was not a knee-jerk response to a world plummeting towards destruction. It wasn't a patch-job or a stop-gap measure. The death of the Son of God was anything but an unexpected peril.

No, it was part of a plan. It was a calculated choice. "It was the LORD's will to crush him." (Isaiah 53:10 NIV) The cross was drawn into the original blueprint. It was written into the script. The moment the forbidden fruit touched the lips of Eve, the shadow of a cross appeared on the horizon. And between that moment and the moment the man with the mallet placed the spike against the wrist of God, a master plan was fulfilled.

What does that mean? It means Jesus planned his own sacrifice.

It means Jesus intentionally planted the tree from which his cross would be carved.

—GOD CAME NEAR

"Look, the Lamb of God, who takes away the *sin* of the *world!*"

—John 1:29 (NIV)

Forget any suggestion that Jesus was trapped. Erase any theory that Jesus made a miscalculation. Ignore any speculation that the cross was a last-ditch attempt to salvage a dying mission.

For if these words tell us anything, they tell us that Jesus died . . . on purpose. No surprise. No hesitation. No faltering.

You can tell a lot about a person by the way he dies. And the way Jesus marched to his death leaves no doubt: he had come to earth for this moment.

Read the words of Peter. "Jesus was given to you, and with the help of those who don't know the law, you put him

to death by nailing him to a cross. But this was God's plan which he had made long ago; he knew all this would happen" (Acts 2:23–24 NCV).

No, the journey to Jerusalem didn't begin in Jericho. It didn't begin in Galilee. It didn't begin in Nazareth. It didn't even begin in Bethlehem. The journey to the cross began long before. As the echo of the crunching of the fruit was still sounding in the garden, Jesus was leaving for Calvary.

—And the Angels Were Silent

The Son went for one last visit with his Father. He met Him in another garden. A garden of gnarled trees and stony soil.

"Does it have to be this way?"

"It does."

"Is there no one else who can do it?"

The King swallowed. "None but you."

"Do I have to drink from the cup?"

"Yes, my Child. The same cup."

He looked at the Prince of Light. "The darkness will be great." He passed his hand over the spotless face of his Son. "The pain will be awful." Then he paused and looked at his darkened dominion. When he looked up, his eyes were moist. "But there is no other way."

The Son looked into the stars as he heard the answer.

"Then, let it be done." Slowly the words that would kill the Son began to come from the lips of the Father.

"Hour of death, moment of sacrifice, it is your moment. Rehearsed a million times on false altars with false lambs, the moment of truth has come.

"Soldiers, you think you lead him? Ropes, you think you bind him? Men, you think you sentence him? He heeds not your commands. He winces not at your lashes. It is my voice he obeys. It is my condemnation he dreads. And it is your souls he saves.

"Oh, my Son, my Child. Look up into the heavens and see my face before I turn it. Hear my voice before I silence it. Would that I could save you and them. But they don't see, and they don't hear.

"The living must die so that the dying can live. The time has come to kill the Lamb.

"Here is the cup, my Son. The cup of sorrows. The cup of sin.

"Slam, mallet! Be true to your task. Let your ring be heard throughout the heavens.

"Lift him, soldiers. Lift him high to his throne of mercy. Lift him up to his perch of death. Lift him above the people that curse his name.

"Now plunge the tree into the earth. Plunge it deep into the heart of humanity. Deep into the strata of time past. Deep into the seeds of time future.

"Is there no angel to save my Isaac? Is there no hand to redeem the Redeemer?

"Here is the cup, my Son. Drink it alone."

God must have wept as he performed his task. Every lie, every lure, every act done in shadows was in that cup. Slowly, hideously they were absorbed into the body of the Son. The final act of incarnation.

The Spotless Lamb was blemished.

—Six Hours One Friday

I can't understand it. I honestly cannot. Why did Jesus do it? Oh, I know, I know. I have heard the official answers. "To gratify the old law." "To fulfill prophecy." And these answers are right. They are. But there is something more here. Something very compassionate. Something yearning. Something personal.

What is it?

I keep thinking of all the people who cast despairing eyes toward the dark heavens and cry "Why?"

And I imagine him. I imagine him listening. I picture his eyes misting and a pierced hand brushing away a tear. And although he may offer no answer, although he may solve no dilemma, although the question may freeze painfully in midair, he who also was once alone, understands.

—No Wonder They Call Him the Savior

His final

prayer

was about you.

His final pain

was for you.

His final

passion

was you.

—And the Angels Were Silent

"Father, *forgive* them; for they ***know*** not what they do."

—Luke 23:34 (KJV)

The cross did what sacrificed lambs could not do. It *erased* our sins, not for a year, but for *eternity*.

—No Wonder They Call Him the Savior

The cross did what man could not do. It granted us the right to talk with, love, and even live with God.

You can't do that by yourself. I don't care how many worship services you attend or good deeds you do, your goodness is insufficient.

You can't be good enough to deserve forgiveness. No one bats a thousand. No one bowls three hundred. No one. Not you, not me, not anyone.

That's why we have guilt in the world.

That's why we need a savior.

You can't forgive me for my sins nor can I forgive you for yours. Two kids in a mud puddle can't clean each other. They need someone clean. Someone spotless. We need someone clean too.

That's why we need a savior.

—No Wonder They Call Him the Savior

Calvary is a hybrid of God's lofty status and his deep devotion. The thunderclap that echoed when God's *sovereignty* collided with his love. The marriage of heaven's *kingship* and heaven's *compassion.* The very instrument of the cross is symbolic, the vertical beam of *holiness* intersecting with the horizontal bar of *love.*

—And the Angels Were Silent

You can't go to the cross with just your head and not your heart. It doesn't work that way. Calvary is not a mental trip. It's not an intellectual exercise. It's not a divine calculation or a cold theological principle.

It's a heart-splitting hour of emotion.

Don't walk away from it dry-eyed and unstirred. Don't just straighten your tie and clear your throat. Don't allow yourself to descend Calvary cool and collected.

Please . . . pause. Look again.

Those are nails in those hands.

That's *God* on that cross.

It's us who put him there.

Peter knew it. John knew it. Mary knew it.

They knew a great price was being paid. They knew who really pierced his side. They also somehow knew that history was being remade.

That's why
they *wept.*

They *saw*
the Savior.

—No Wonder They Call Him the Savior

For the *joy* set before
him he endured the *cross,*
scorning its shame, and sat
down at the right hand of
the *throne* of God.

—Hebrews 12:2 (NIV)